ABOUT THE AUTHORS

It is thanks to **Eileen Dover**, the queen of investigative journalists, that we know that Robert Maxwell was nick-named Tarzan because he was always yelling and liked to be surrounded by creepers. She exposed to us, too, that he used to send his mother a congratulatory telegram every year – on *his* birthday. And it was Eileen Dover who unearthed what is, to date, the most grisly secret of the fat crook's past – that he has two half-brothers and a half-sister, and it might have been worse if his mother had not got the chainsaw off him.

A consultant anologist, **Seymour Fish** has devoted his life to the study of arseholes. 'Maxwell was the most perfect one I've ever met,' he says. 'He did for employee relations what President Truman did for Hiroshima. He was so devious he could go in a revolving door behind you – and come out before you.' In a letter to *The Lancet* in 1990, Dr Fish penned the prophetic words: 'Robert Maxwell is lower than whaleshit – and that's at the bottom of the ocean.'

Other joint publications by Eileen Dover & Seymour Fish

A DROP IN THE RATINGS:
THE OFFICIAL JEREMY BEADLE JOKE BOOK

A DROP IN THE FREQUENCY WITH WHICH I AM INVITED TO
TEA AT BUCKINGHAM PALACE:
THE OFFICIAL ANDREW MORTON JOKE BOOK

EILEEN DOVER & SEYMOUR FISH

A DROP IN THE OCEAN

The official Robert Maxwell Joke Book

Profusely illustrated by John Kent

CORGI BOOKS

A DROP IN THE OCEAN: THE OFFICIAL ROBERT MAXWELL JOKE BOOK
A CORGI BOOK 0 552 14035 X

First publication in Great Britain

PRINTING HISTORY
Corgi edition published 1992

Copyright © Transworld Publishers 1992

Capt. Bob cartoon strip copyright © John Kent
(reproduced by kind permission of John Kent and *Private Eye*)

Corgi Books are published by Transworld Publishers Ltd, 61-63 Uxbridge Road, London
W5 5SA, in Australia by Transworld Publishers (Australia) Pty Ltd, 15-23 Helles Avenue,
Moorebank, NSW 2170, and in New Zealand by Transworld Publishers (NZ) Ltd, 3 William
Pickering Drive, Albany, Auckland.

Printed and bound in Great Britain by
Cox & Wyman Ltd, Reading, Berks.

For all those who suffered at the hands of Robert Maxwell

Great Helmsman Overboard!
Robert is dead and gone away;
No longer bound by common clay
He's shuffled off this mortal coil –
Turned into Mount of Olives oil;
And though no longer full of beans
He'll grace a tin of small sardines.

(Sent by an anonymous *Daily Mirror* reader
to Michael White of the *Guardian* after his remark,
'It shows there is a God after all!')

ACKNOWLEDGEMENTS

The publishers of this book would like to thank the following:

Martyn Forrester, whose idea it was in the first place.

Mark 'Boy' Lucas, for waiving his usually extortionate agent's fees.

John Kent, for kind permission to use his brilliant *Capt. Bob* cartoon strip.

Dave Cash and the *Private Eye* team, for their support.

Andrew Esson, for his nice bit of graffito.

Alan Sampson and his colleagues at Little, Brown (ex-Maxwell employees), for trying.

Michael White of the *Guardian*, for being in the right place at the right time.

Steve Hitchman, Michael Geare, Mike Styles, Richard Craig and **George Thaw**, for the true stories.

Knock, knock.
Who's there?
Betty.
Betty who?
Betty jumped!

What does MIRROR stand for?
Must Invest in Rubber Ring Or Raft.

What's the difference between Popeye and
Robert Maxwell?
Popeye got to Mount Olive before he died.

Did you hear that Robert Maxwell finally
achieved his lifelong ambition?
He became a pier.

What did Mrs Maxwell say to her husband on
the fateful last night?
*'Sure, Bob, have another drink – just don't go
overboard.'*

TRUE STORY

A surprise party was arranged on the helicopter
pad on the roof of the *Mirror* building by editors
who wanted to celebrate Robert Maxwell's
birthday. But on the day, on his instructions,
security was revised to restrict access to the
roof. Editors had to run from one side of the
building to the other and back again, and use
three separate lifts. They arrived just in time for
Maxwell, who had already helped himself liberally
to food and drink, to call them fools and take off
in a gale of downwash which bowled over the
table holding opened champagne bottles and
canapés.

What's the difference between Robert Maxwell
and Maxwell House?
Maxwell House dissolves in water.

What's the difference between Robert Maxwell and an Essex Girl?
An Essex girl won't slip off yer boat. (Boat race = face)

How did they discover that Robert Maxwell was gay?
They found him clinging to a buoy.

What's long and brown and goes *ffsssst?*
Robert Maxwell's last cigar.

How could Robert Maxwell have been saved?
You mean you care?

Did you hear, they've finally found out what happened to Robert Maxwell? Apparently he used to invite prostitutes aboard to keep him company when he was cruising. On this particular night the one he picked was Irish, and like an idiot, he asked her to toss him off...

TRUE STORY

In the early 1960s, Robert Maxwell, then owner of Pergamon Press and a Labour MP, found himself chairman of a Publishers' Association committee.

Members of the committee were subjected to some bizarre conditions during their meetings. Present on one occasion, for example, at Maxwell's room in the House of Commons, was a Chief Constable in whose county the fat crook was being prosecuted for driving on a motorway while using an electric shaver. At other meetings Maxwell chaired, he also dictated to his secretary while taking and making telephone calls.

For some of the committee members the final straw came when they saw the draft of the report that Maxwell had produced on their behalf.

'Mr Maxwell,' their spokesman, Michael Turner, announced, 'I have to tell you that some of us wish to submit a minority report.'

'What?!' the fat man fumed. 'What's wrong

with my report?'

'Nothing, in broad terms. It's just that whilst agreeing in principle with the contents of the report, we wish to be dissociated from its grammar and syntax.'

A few days later, Turner was summoned to Pergamon HQ.

'I want you to know something,' Maxwell exploded angrily as Turner entered his room. 'I've got your name, and I'll tell you this: you'll never work in publishing again.'

It is a matter of history that Michael Turner went on to become Chief Executive of ABP (Associated Book Publishers) and President of the Publishers' Association.

Why didn't Robert Maxwell have a shower on the *Lady Ghislaine*?
He preferred to wash up on shore.

You know what's next door to the Ted Kennedy Driving School?
The shop where they sell Robert Maxwell water wings.

What did they do when they found that Robert Maxwell was too big for his coffin?

They gave him an enema and put him in a shoebox.

Why didn't the *Lady Ghislaine*'s captain insist on Robert Maxwell wearing a life jacket?

He knew that turds floated.

What was the last thing Robert Maxwell said to his wife?

'You check the dogs, darling, I'll feed the fish.'

What's worse than finding glass in your baby food?

Finding Robert Maxwell in your tuna fish salad.

The newly deceased arrived in heaven and, on being asked his name, replied: 'Maxwell. Robert Maxwell.'

The angel on the gate looked into his ledger and said, 'I'm sorry, but I can't find an appointment for you. What was your business on earth?'

'Head of Maxwell Communications Corporation,' Maxwell said.

'I'll go and enquire,' said the angel, but when he returned the fat man was gone. And so were the Pearly Gates.

Why would Paddy Ashdown like to talk to Robert Maxwell?
Because he's a floating voter.

What was Robert Maxwell's favourite chocolate bar?
Drifter.

What was Robert Maxwell's favourite game?
Squash.

One night aboard the *Lady Ghislaine* Robert Maxwell couldn't sleep. He went out on deck and started hallucinating that he was chatting to Rupert Murdoch and Kerry Packer. Pretty soon Rupert Murdoch said, 'If you'll excuse me, nature calls.' He jumped off the boat and walked across the water to a toilet ashore on the Canaries.

A few minutes after he had rejoined Maxwell and Packer, Packer excused himself for the same reason, jumped off the boat, and walked across the water to the shore. When he returned, Robert Maxwell marvelled at what they both had done. He couldn't help wondering if they had special God-given powers, and as his own bladder filled up he pondered whether, as a fellow media baron, he might have the same special powers himself. So he stood up and excused himself, stepped overboard, and sank like a stone. Splashing and struggling to the surface, he yelled, 'Help me, oh God – you helped them, so help me!'

Murdoch and Packer looked at each other, and Murdoch said, 'Do you think we should tell him about the rocks?'

A certain Mr Maxwell was sent by his company to Africa to sell refrigerators. When he had settled in at his hotel, he sent a telegram to his wife, as he knew she'd be worried about him.

Unfortunately the telegram was delivered to the wrong Mrs Maxwell, and arrived the day after her husband had jumped ship. It read: 'Arrived safely. The heat is terrible.'

The day after Robert Maxwell died, one of the deceased media baron's personal staff phoned the *Daily Telegraph*.

'I want to print an announcement that Mr Maxwell's died,' she said. 'Nothing expensive, mind. We haven't any money. Just something like, "Maxwell's dead".'

'There's a minimum charge for up to five words, madam,' said the man at the *Telegraph*. 'You might as well add another three words and get value for money.'

'All right then,' said the employee, thinking for a moment. 'Maxwell's dead. Boat for sale.'

TRUE STORY

Vienna, 1946. A war-torn city of transit camps and refugees and shadowy people who are up to no good. Second or third in charge of the region's railway system, which is at the very hub of the transportation of people and goods from West to East and vice versa, is a young and dashing British Army captain who answers to the name of Robert Maxwell MC.

In the early hours of a snowy winter morning, an eastbound train pulls into Vienna. It is en route from Leipzig to Moscow with a valuable cargo of rare books, looted by the Nazis during the time of their occupation, and now being returned to their rightful owners, the Soviet people. It is an important consignment, so Robert Maxwell MC obtains all the relevant documentation from the guard and takes it back to his office for 'processing'. Two hours later he reappears. There has been a change of plan, he announces: the cargo is being re-routed westwards to London. What is more, the name and address of the consignee have been changed, but the guard does not question it. After all, in his capacity at the rail yard, Captain Robert Maxwell MC is a representative of the British government.

History does not relate whether Mr Maxwell enjoyed reading the books that were delivered to the house of one of his friends, but what is clear is that the proceeds from their sale were enough to set him up for life.

What was Robert Maxwell's favourite bird?
Robin.

What was Robert Maxwell's favourite instrument?
The lute.

When Robert Maxwell was born, he was so fat and ugly that the doctor slapped his mother.

Why did Robert Maxwell jump overboard?
  He wanted to loot the sandbank.

What do you call an overweight newspaper proprietor floating upside down in the Atlantic Ocean?
  Hugely funny.

How do you save an overweight newspaper proprietor from drowning?
  If you don't know, I'm certainly not going to tell you.

What do you get if you cross Robert Maxwell with a flying fish?
  Flat sailors.

What was Robert Maxwell's favourite pudding?
   Sue-it.

Did you hear Robert Maxwell was busted coming through Customs?
   They looked in the back of his underpants and found three hundred pounds of crack.

What's the difference between Robert Maxwell and a dictionary of business ethics?
   About 30,000 words.

How come Robert Maxwell floated?
   Scum always rises.

A Maxwell director returned from a long trip to the States, having left his beloved cat in his secretary's care. The minute he'd cleared Customs, he called her up and enquired after his pet.

'Your cat's dead,' replied his secretary bluntly.

The director was devastated. 'You know how much that cat meant to me,' he moaned into the phone. 'Couldn't you at least have thought of a nicer way of breaking the news? Couldn't you have said, "Well, you know, the cat got out of the house one day and climbed up on to the roof, and the fire brigade couldn't get him down, and finally he died of exposure"? Why are you always so thoughtless?'

'Look, I'm sorry,' said his secretary. 'I'll try to do better next time.'

'OK, let's just put it behind us. How are you, anyway? And how's Cap'n Bob?'

The secretary was silent for a moment. 'Er,' she stammered, 'I'm fine and I think Mr Maxwell's gone swimming.'

What's the definition of mixed emotions?
When you see Robert Maxwell fall off his yacht clutching your pay cheque.

TRUE STORIES

Just after Robert Maxwell took over the *Daily Mirror* it was the fiftieth anniversary of the *Old Codgers* column. The editor of the column wrote a memo to Maxwell saying that it would be a generous gesture if the new proprietor sent a bottle of champagne and a message to the staff. Nothing happened until months after the event, when a bemused secretary turned up to hand over a bottle of Cordon Rouge, the cheapest in the Mumm range. There was no message attached to the bottle, which turned out to have been donated to Maxwell by a sycophantic supplier hoping for some business.

Robert Maxwell got a letter from the blood transfusion service asking him to become a blood donor. His secretary wrote back that he wasn't even a blood owner.

'And here,' said the captain, pointing at a brass plaque on the deck, 'is where Robert Maxwell fell.'

'I'm not surprised,' said the coroner, 'I nearly tripped over it myself.'

What's the difference between Robert Maxwell and a photocopying machine?
One makes facsimiles, the other makes sick families.

What's the difference between Robert Maxwell and the Royal Navy?
One rules the waves, the other waives the rules.

Robert Maxwell was outraged at being searched by Customs on his arrival at JFK. 'New York is the arsehole of the world!' he screamed.

'Yessir,' said the Customs official. 'And I take it you're just passing through?'

Robert Maxwell went to a girlfriend's flat one night and found her sitting naked in front of the mirror, admiring her breasts.

'What do you think you're doing?' he asked.

'I went to the doctor today,' she said, 'and he told me I have beautiful breasts.'

'Oh yeah? And what did he have to say about your fat flabby ass?'

'Nothing,' she replied. 'Your name wasn't mentioned at all.'

Robert Maxwell was stark naked in front of the open window, doing his morning aerobics. A lady friend entered the room and suddenly rushed over and closed the curtains. 'Bob, you fool!' she shouted. 'I don't want the neighbours to think I only love you for your money!'

What do you get if you cross Robert Maxwell with a cement mixer?
A hardened criminal.

TRUE STORY

In the late 1960s, Robert Maxwell was pontificating at a meeting of the Publishers' Association on the various merits of publishing fiction or non-fiction.

'Under no circumstances whatsoever,' the fat man frothed, 'would *I* ever contemplate publishing fiction.'

'Is that so?' called out Anthony Blond from the floor. 'Then what about your balance sheet?'

What do you get if you cross Robert Maxwell with an ocean?
   A crime wave.

What's the similarity between Robert Maxwell and an Essex girl?
   Both went down in Tenerife.

Contrary to malicious rumour, Robert Maxwell did balance his company budgets perfectly. The money he owed was exactly the same amount as the money he had stolen.

'I made five hundred dollars last night,' said one New York hooker to another.
   'Gross?' the other asked.
   'Certainly was: Robert Maxwell.'

Why was it Robert Maxwell's wish to be put in his coffin face down?
   So all his employees could kiss him goodbye.

Robert Maxwell was once arrested at the Christmas party for picking his way through the crowd – a pocket at a time.

What was Robert Maxwell's last nickname?
Cap'n Bob, bob, bob.

NEWSFLASH:
*Maxwell missing. Japanese whaling
fleet suspected.*

NEWSFLASH:
*False alarm. Coastguard not sighted Maxwell after
all. It was Gibraltar.*

Robert Maxwell was treading water, surrounded by a school of man-eating sharks. They circled him menacingly, ready to make their strike.

'Who's going first?' one shark asked.

As is usual for sharks, the leader went up to the fat man and sniffed him before going in for the kill. He returned to the others with a sad expression on his face. 'We can't eat him, lads,' he said, 'he's one of us.'

What did Robert Maxwell get for Christmas?
  Fat.

How do we know that Robert Maxwell was fat?
  The newspapers said the crew of the Lady
  Ghislaine *always gave him a wide berth.*

What did Robert Maxwell's autopsy prove?
  That he had huge amounts of guts.

Have you heard, the Canary Islands have been
sighted off the coast of Maxwell?

Name a deadly poison.
  Lady Ghislaine – *one drop and you're dead.*

Robert Maxwell once said that he had bought a
suit for a ridiculous price. Actually, he'd bought
it for an absurd figure.

What were Robert Maxwell's final words?
   'Glug, glug.'

Why is the water in the Canary Islands so
wholesome?
   Because it's full of body.

What did the captain of the *Lady Ghislaine* say
when he sighted Robert Maxwell?
   'A vast behind!'

How could you have made a small fortune on
Maxwell shares?
   By starting with a large one.

What did Robert Maxwell fall against when he
fell off the boat?
   His will. (Believe that and you'll believe anything.)

TRUE STORY

One unfortunate consultant who was used a lot by Robert Maxwell received a phone call from his employer a week before the Christmas holiday.

'I want to talk to you about something,' Maxwell said, 'but the only free time I have is at 11 a.m. on Christmas morning.'

'That's a little inconvenient,' the consultant explained. 'I mean, you live a hundred miles away from my house, and Christmas Day is, after all, a family occasion. '

Maxwell ranted and raved to such an extent that the man realized his future employment was in jeopardy, and he reluctantly agreed to attend the meeting. He duly arrived at Headington Hall at five minutes to eleven on Christmas Day, after driving one hundred miles in terrible weather conditions.

'Ah yes, I'm so glad you came,' Maxwell beamed from the doorstep, without inviting him in. 'There was something important I wanted to tell you. You're fired.'

Why did Robert Maxwell kill himself in the Canaries?

To avoid doing bird.

How do we know Robert Maxwell was such a crook?

He even double-crossed the Atlantic.

What do you call Robert Maxwell floating in the ocean?

Anything you like, he can't hear you.

When one City banker heard that Robert Maxwell was offering shares in Maxwell Communications as collateral for his loans, he remarked: 'Hmm, a bit like airlifting passengers off the *Titanic* in the *Hindenberg*.'

How was the trade in Maxwell shares the day
before they were suspended?
*Chugging along slowly, with a big
drop-off overnight.*

There were two schools of thought about
Robert Maxwell. People either hated him, or
absolutely loathed him.

Some liked Maxwell's approach. Most preferred
his departure.

PLAQUE ON ROBERT MAXWELL'S DESK:
*'It's no longer the principle that counts, it's
the interest.'*

Did you hear that Robert Maxwell died of
RAIDS?
Recently Acquired Income Deficiency Syndrome.

A *Sunday Times* journalist goes to the doctor and the doctor says, 'Sit down, I have some terribly bad news to tell you. The results of your tests have come in from the lab, and I'm afraid I have to tell you that you only have six months to live.'

'Good God!' the journalist exclaims, 'that's horrible!'

The doctor says, 'Yes, but I have some advice for you. I think you should leave the *Sunday Times* and go and work for Robert Maxwell.'

'Is that going to save me?' the journalist says.

'No,' the doctor replies, 'but it will be the longest six months you ever lived.'

ROBERT MAXWELL TO SECRETARY:
Get me my broker on the telephone.
SECRETARY:
Yes, sir. Stock or pawn?

TRUE STORY

At a board meeting of one of his many subsidiary companies, Robert Maxwell was roasting a manager who had committed a fairly minor error of judgement. He effed and blinded as only he could, for close to half an hour, calling the poor man every name under the sun. Finally, just when his fit of rage seemed to have abated, he shouted at the man, 'Stand up! Come on, stand up!'

'Right,' Maxwell fulminated at the cowering figure. 'And now say, "I am a fucking cunt." '

The manager, who was a perfect Maxwell employee – big mortgage, children at expensive schools – had little choice but to comply.

What did Robert Maxwell's mistress and the Atlantic Ocean have in common?
They both swallowed newspaper proprietors.

The first thing Robert Maxwell did when he got to hell was to set up the *Daily Sinner* in competition with heaven's *Guardian Angel*.

One day he ran a nasty piece about God and, quick as a flash, St Peter was on the phone.

'You print a retraction right now,' St Peter demanded, 'or we'll sue.'

'I don't think so,' the fat man said confidently. 'I've got all the lawyers.'

It was Maxwell's boast that he always did the opposite of what his advisers suggested. And before he embarked on his final trip on the *Lady Ghislaine*, they united in telling him not to make waves . . .

Why did Robert Maxwell wear a baseball cap?
  So he'd know which end to wipe.

This nice journalist dies and goes to heaven, where he is shown to a simple hut, dressed in a humble robe, and offered wine and cheese. He had rather anticipated something a little more luxurious, but all his needs are catered for and he settles in happily. Until, that is, on his daily stroll, he comes across Robert Maxwell. The fat man is dressed in fabulous robes, lounging on a fur-lined cloud with a gorgeous mistress, and is holding a bottle of the finest vintage port.

Somewhat miffed, the journalist goes to St Peter and says, 'Look, mate, on earth I was a good guy, never hurt a fly, never lied, cheated or stole, and all I get in heaven is a hut, a simple robe and a bottle of cheap plonk. And there's this guy who stole from his employees, lied to whole nations, and generally caused more misery and hardship than just about any other man who ever lived, and he's in the lap of absolute luxury. It's not fair!'

'I'm not as daft as I appear to be, my son,' smiles St Peter. 'You see, he's been given a bottle of port with a hole in it and a mistress without one.'

MAXWELL'S GRANDSON:
Grandad, do you know how to croak?
ROBERT MAXWELL:
I don't think so, why?
GRANDSON:
Because Dad says he'll be rich when you do.

ROBERT MAXWELL TO DOCTOR:
I haven't been myself lately.
DOCTOR:
Sounds like you're a lot better.

What did Robert Maxwell's mistress and Tottenham Hotspur have in common?
He pulled out of both of them.

Kevin and Ian Maxwell are walking down the road with their lawyer when they encounter a friend. They introduce the two men to each other, and after the introductions Kevin takes the friend to one side and says, 'You know, this lawyer is brilliant but there's something really weird about him, he's got two arseholes.'

'Two arseholes?' says the friend. 'How do you know that?'

'Because every time we walk into the Court of Appeal the policeman at the door says, "Here comes that brilliant lawyer with the two arseholes!" '

Did you ever see Robert Maxwell's new shoes?
    Neither did he.

Why did Robert Maxwell have such a small willy?
    Nothing grows in the shade.

TRUE STORY

Robert Maxwell liked to show off his Oxfordshire home, Headington Hall, to each and every visitor. One day he was taking *Daily Telegraph* editor Max Hastings on a conducted tour when he pointed to an enormous stained-glass window.

'I'll bet you a bottle of my finest champagne you can't tell me what biblical scene that window depicts,' Maxwell challenged.

Without hesitation, Hastings replied: 'Samson at the gates of Gaza.'

'Somebody must have told you!' exclaimed an angry Maxwell.

'Not at all,' said Hastings. 'Just one of the benefits of a good education.'

Maxwell was not happy, but as he disappeared downstairs he said, 'Don't worry, I always pay my debts.'

A couple of minutes later he came back up, and presented Max Hastings with a can of Carlsberg.

Did you hear about the all-expenses-paid vacation for losers?

Grace Kelly drives you to the airport, Ted Kennedy picks you up at the other end, Robert Maxwell takes you boating, and Roman Polanski stays home and looks after your kids.

What do you need when you have a newspaper baron up to his neck in shit?
More shit.

Where was Robert Maxwell's sex organ?
In his feet. If he stepped on you, you were screwed.

'Is this pig?' said a furious Robert Maxwell at a publishing dinner, holding up a piece of meat on his fork and waving it about angrily.

'Depends which end of the fork you're referring to,' came the brave reply.

While Robert Maxwell was out at lunch one day, half a dozen of his top executives met in the boardroom at Maxwell House to work out some way of easing the fat man out of the driver's seat.

But suddenly the secretary of one of the executives burst into the room and said, 'He's back!'

'My God,' said an executive, 'if he catches us here he'll know what we're up to. Quick, there's no time to lose. Five of us will have to jump out of the window.'

'But we're on the thirteenth floor,' protested a colleague.

'Jump!' insisted the other. 'This is no time for superstition.'

TRUE STORY

When holding dinner parties in his Holborn flat, Robert Maxwell always insisted on full sample menus, and would often eat a three-course trial meal before sitting down with his guests!

Robert Maxwell was a hard-headed character who seldom admitted a doubt about the value of his opinions.

Finally, a braver-than-most newspaper editor buttonholed him at a cocktail party and said, 'You always think you're right, don't you, Maxwell? But there must have been times when you've been wrong, admit it.'

'Well, yes,' confessed Maxwell. 'I was wrong once.'

'When was that?'

'Well,' intoned the fat man, 'some years back I made an important decision which I thought was wrong, but in the end it wasn't.'

GRAFFITO ON LOO WALL AT PERGAMON PRESS, CIRCA 1980:

Working for Bob is like smoking marijuana. The harder you suck, the higher you get.

The inspector from the Inland Revenue once had a tip for Robert Maxwell.

'The trick,' he wrote to the proprietor of Pergamon Press, 'is to stop thinking of it as *your* money.'

Robert Maxwell was notoriously jealous of other big tycoons, and he was mightily put out when Rupert Murdoch called him one day in the early 80s on the new-fangled cellular phone he'd just had installed in his Rolls-Royce.

Furious that he'd been left behind in the technology race, he immediately had the highest-tech phone known to man installed in his car and called Murdoch later that evening.

'Hi Rupert,' he said breezily, 'just thought I'd call you back and ask you if *your* car-phone has a fifty-number memory and hands-free operation?'

'Yes,' Murdoch replied, 'but can you hang on for a second – I'm wanted on the other line...'

What did MCC stand for?
Mushroom Communications Corporation. The employees were kept in the dark and fed shit.

Ivan was in charge of a big publishing project in downtown Stalingrad just after the war and his first task was to take bids from international publishers for the job. His first interview was with a representative from Warsaw.

'You've seen the brief,' Ivan said. 'How much will you charge to get the job done?'

'Two hundred thousand dollars,' said the Pole.

'Not bad,' said Ivan. 'What's the breakdown?'

'One hundred thousand for materials, one hundred thousand for labour.'

'OK,' said Ivan, making a note of the bid and showing him the door. 'I'll be in touch.'

The next interview was with an American, who came up with a bid for four hundred thousand dollars. 'Half for materials,' he explained, 'half for labour.'

'That's a little steep,' said Ivan, 'but I'll get back to you.'

The third bid came from Robert Maxwell of Pergamon Press. 'Six hundred thousand dollars,' said the fat man emphatically.

'Jesus, that's astronomical!' exclaimed Ivan. 'Could you break that down for me?'

'Sure,' said Maxwell. 'Two hundred grand for me, two hundred grand for you, and two hundred grand for the Pole.'

TRUE STORY

Sunday Times financial journalist Ivan Fallon invited Robert Maxwell to a power lunch one day, but, just as Fallon and his other guests were going to their table, Maxwell telephoned to cancel.

'I'm sorry, I really can't make it,' the fat man said. 'I had some urgent business to attend to, and I am in Bucharest.'

Fallon said not to worry, these things happened, he quite understood. 'You're missing an excellent get-together, though,' he added, and went on to list the distinguished guests, who included some of the top banking names in the City.

'Hold on a moment,' Maxwell said.

There was a brief silence, and then the fat man came back on the line. 'I'll be round in ten minutes,' he said.

Robert Maxwell was giving one of his employees a lecture. 'In business,' he said, 'ethics are very important. For instance, suppose you are running a small business and a customer comes in and settles a £20 account in cash. Just after he's left, you notice that he's given you two £20 notes stuck together. Immediately, you are faced with a basic ethical question: should I tell my partner?'

When Maxwell called in an industrial psychologist to give his employees the once-over, he insisted on taking the tests himself.

The psychologist found the chairman's responses most enlightening, especially one:

Question: What is your usual reaction to criticism?

Answer: Extreme surprise.

The lawyer brought a very long and complex contract he'd written to show Robert Maxwell. After the fat man had been reading for some time, he looked up and said, 'It's a pity your work doesn't have a wider readership. Your small print is superb.'

What did the stockbroker say to the client to get him to buy Maxwell shares?

'Go on, take the plunge.'

Nicolae Ceausescu arrives in hell and is shown around the place. When passing a row of pits, each filled with unspeakable slime and filth, he sees several other famous swindlers and crooks. Emil Savundra is submerged up to his neck in evil slurry. But Al Capone, next in line, is only up to his ankles.

'Hey,' the dead dictator says to Lucifer, 'are you going soft or something? How come Capone gets off so lightly?'

'It's not as bad as it seems,' says the Devil. 'He's standing on Robert Maxwell's shoulders.'

Robert Maxwell was the sort of man who would have taken a taxi to the bankruptcy court, then invited the driver in as a creditor.

TRUE STORY

Robert Maxwell was lunching at the Savoy Hotel with a group of top businessmen when he summoned a waiter and asked for a telephone to be brought to the table.

'I'd be grateful if you could keep the noise down for a minute,' Maxwell announced to his fellow diners, producing a piece of paper from his pocket and dialling a long-distance number.

'Ronald?' he boomed into the phone. 'It's Bob here. Yes, I'm fine thanks. How's Nancy? Good. Now listen, about what we were talking about last night. I've been in touch with Mikhail and I think I'll be able to swing it for you. I shall be going to Number 10 in a few minutes' time to bring the Prime Minister up to date, and then I'll fly to Geneva to handle the talks myself. No, don't thank me, it's a pleasure. Yes, sure, I'll keep in touch.'

The assembled heads of industry looked on in amazement as Maxwell put down the receiver, made his excuses, and left.

In his haste to leave, however, Maxwell left behind the piece of paper with the telephone number he had dialled. Unable to contain his curiosity, one of the businessmen picked it up and dialled the number when he got back to his office.

It was the talking clock in New York.

ROBERT MAXWELL:
Doctor! Doctor! I keep stealing money from my employees' pension funds.
DOCTOR:
Have you taken anything for it?

Robert Maxwell once had to leave the country before finding out the result of one of his many libel suits. His lawyer promised to let him know the verdict as soon as it was announced. A week later, Maxwell received a fax which simply said, 'Justice has triumphed!' Maxwell immediately faxed back his reply: 'Appeal at once!'

EXCERPT FROM A LETTER FROM ROBERT MAXWELL TO NATWEST:

'If you could see your way to giving me an overdraft I will be forever in your debt.'

'We'd like to give you the extended loan you're asking for,' said the manager of NatWest to Robert Maxwell, 'but what assurance can you give that it will be repaid on time?'

'Won't a gentleman's word of honour do?' asked Maxwell.

'Of course,' said the bank manager. 'When will you be bringing him in?'

How many Maxwells does it take to screw in a lightbulb?

None of your bloody business, and if you persist in asking we'll sue.

What do you call a man who steals from pension funds?

Rob.

Why is it good that newspaper tycoons have mistresses to screw?

So for twenty minutes they'll stop screwing everyone else.

Getting out of a cab one evening, Robert Maxwell gave the driver a fifty-pence tip. The cabbie looked at it disdainfully and said that one of Maxwell's sons had given him five times as much only the night before.

'That may be so,' said Maxwell. 'But my son has a millionaire for a father, I haven't.'

Robert Maxwell was in court for running an old man over, a charge that he strenuously denied. 'Then tell us how you came to get a puncture in your tyre?' said the judge.

'I drove over a milk bottle,' said Maxwell.

'So you didn't see the milk bottle lying in the road?'

'How could I? That stupid pensioner had it hidden under his coat.'

ROBERT MAXWELL:
  Doctor, doctor, how can I get rid of twenty-eight pounds of ugly fat?
DOCTOR:
  Cut off your head.

Robert Maxwell once assembled his entire staff to tell them a new joke he'd just heard. Naturally, everyone present roared with laughter when he'd finished, apart from one independent soul.

'What's the matter with you?' spat Maxwell. 'Didn't you think the joke was funny?'

'I don't have to laugh,' said the man. 'I'm leaving on Friday anyway.'

Why were there so many sad women in Czechoslovakia after the Second World War?

Because the biggest prick emigrated to England.

A lady friend of Robert Maxwell's went to her doctor for a once-over.

'When was the last time you had a check-up?' the doctor asked.

'That's a bit personal,' said the lady, 'but if you must know it was last night.'

Robert Maxwell travelled all the way to Rome and got himself an audience with the Pope. As soon as the two were alone together, he leaned over and whispered, 'Your Holiness, I have an offer I think might interest you. I'm in a position to give you a million pounds if you'll change the wording in the Lord's Prayer from "give us each day our daily bread" to "give us each day our *Daily Mirror*". Now, what do you say?'

'Absolutely not!' said the shocked Holy Father.

'OK, I understand, it's a big decision,' said Maxwell. 'How about five million pounds?'

'I couldn't contemplate it,' said the Pope.

'Look, I know it's a tough one,' Maxwell insisted. 'Tell you what, I'll go all the way up to fifty million pounds.'

Asking him to leave the room, the Pope called in his cardinals and whispered, 'When is it exactly that our contract with Mother's Pride expires?'

MAXWELL COMMUNICATIONS GROUP PERSONNEL DIRECTOR TO JOB APPLICANT:
'Not only do we have an excellent retirement plan, but if you come to work here you'll find you age a lot faster.'

At an international doctors' convention in Switzerland a conversation was taking place in a restaurant after the day's seminars were over. An Israeli doctor said, 'Medicine in my country is so advanced that we can take a kidney out of one person and put it in another and have him looking for work in six weeks.'

A German doctor said, 'That's nothing. In Germany we can take a lung out of one person and put it in someone else and have him looking for work in four weeks.'

A Russian doctor said, 'In my country, medicine is so advanced that we can take half a heart from one person, put it in another, and have them both looking for work in two weeks.'

The British doctor said, 'That's nothing. In Britain we can take an arsehole out of Czechoslovakia, put him in Fleet Street, and have half the publishing industry looking for work the next day.'

What do you call Robert Maxwell near a pension fund?

Thief!

Robert Maxwell, formerly Jan Ludwig Hoch, had a bit of trouble learning English and understanding our ways when he first came over from Czechoslovakia. One day he saw a poster outside a police station saying MAN WANTED FOR ROBBERY and so he went in and applied.

JOURNALIST TO ROBERT MAXWELL AT
CHRISTMAS PARTY:
*What's the difference between a rectum and an
arsehole?*
MAXWELL:
*I don't know. What is the difference between a
rectum and an arsehole?*
JOURNALIST, PUTTING HIS ARM AROUND
MAXWELL'S SHOULDERS:
You can't put your arm around a rectum.

Three doctors were sitting around drinking coffee one morning after an early session of operations.

'I reckon the operation I performed this morning was the easiest ever,' said the first doctor.

'Bet mine was easier,' said the second doctor.

'I'd put any money on the fact that mine was the easiest,' said the third.

'I don't know about that,' said the first doctor. 'I operated on a German engineer.'

'I operated on a Japanese electronics expert,' said the second.

'I operated on a Czech newspaper proprietor,' said the third.

'German engineers have got to be the easiest,' said the first doctor. 'You open them up and they have wheels and cogs inside, all neatly numbered. You simply change a part and close.'

The second doctor said, 'You're wrong. Japanese electronics experts are definitely the easiest to operate on. They have colour-coded transistors and microchips; you just change a defective component and you're done.'

'You're both wrong,' said the third doctor. 'Czech newspaper proprietors are by far the easiest to operate on. They've only got two moving parts, the mouth and the arsehole – and they're interchangeable.'

MCC FIRST AID INSTRUCTOR TO
EMPLOYEE:
   What telephone number would you dial if the
   chairman had a heart attack?
EMPLOYEE:
   998.

Robert Maxwell and a fellow Czech were
camping together in the wilds of Canada when
suddenly two bears appeared. Before they could
make a run for it, one of the bears grabbed
Maxwell's friend. Robert Maxwell, scared out of
his wits, made his escape and ran back towards
town. He found a Mountie, told him the story,
and the two of them hurried back to the
campsite.

   When they got there, the two bears, a male
and a female, were still sitting around, but the
Czech had gone. The Mountie said, 'Which of
the bears ate the Czech?'

   'That one,' said the newspaper proprietor,
'the male.'

   So the Mountie shot the male bear, but when
they cut him open his stomach was empty.

   And the moral of the story is: Never trust a
newspaper proprietor who says the Czech is in
the male.

Robert Maxwell's business career was phenomenal. He started off a barefoot peasant dressed in rags and became one of the most highly suspected figures in the City.

'How do I stand?' Robert Maxwell asked his doctor.

'I don't know,' said the doctor. 'To me, it's a miracle.'

When Kevin Maxwell was little he once got an empty box for Christmas. His father told him it was an Action Man deserter.

Another Christmas, Robert Maxwell went outside with his gun and fired a shot into the air. A few minutes later he came back inside and told his sons that Santa Claus had committed suicide.

How did the rescue authorities manage to locate Robert Maxwell's body?
They followed the trail of half-eaten sharks.

Soon after buying the *Daily Mirror*, Robert Maxwell walked into the building and said: 'This is my son Kevin. He's going to start at the bottom for a few days.'

When Ian Maxwell was at school, his teacher asked him: 'If your father borrowed one hundred pounds from you and promised to pay it back at ten pounds a week, how much would he owe you at the end of nine weeks?'
'One hundred pounds,' said Ian.
'You don't know your arithmetic,' scolded the teacher.
'You don't know my father,' said Ian.

Did you hear that Robert Maxwell bequeathed his body to medical science?

Medical science is contesting the will.

'You're overweight,' Robert Maxwell's doctor once told him after a check-up.

'I demand a second opinion,' said Maxwell.

'All right, then,' the doctor said. 'You're ugly as well.'

One Derby County supporter was so upset by Robert Maxwell's activities that after a particularly bad match he muscled his way into the directors' box and punched Maxwell square on the jaw.

The incident is still fondly remembered in the town as the day the fan hit the shit.

The heart transplant unit at Papworth Hospital were desperate to get hold of Robert Maxwell's heart after his death. Apparently it's not often they can get one that's hardly been used.

TRUE STORY

On his way to the Labour Party conference at Brighton one year, Robert Maxwell spotted a fish and chip shop and ordered his driver to stop. Instructing his companion, a PR man, to go in and buy five fish suppers, he then, to everyone's amazement, proceeded to scoff the lot. When he had finished, he crumpled up the greasy newspapers and threw them out of the window of the moving Rolls. They landed on the windscreen of the police car behind, whose occupants were deeply unimpressed. Pulling Maxwell's car over, the policemen pointed out that not only was the fat man in breach of the litter laws, but that his actions might have seriously endangered the lives of other road users.

'You know who I am, officer,' Maxwell said, 'and I totally agree with you. This man here is responsible, and when I arrive at the conference I will fire him immediately.'

Robert Maxwell hired a new lawyer and said: 'I'll give you £100,000 if you do the worrying for me.'

'Fine,' said the lawyer. 'Now, where's the £100,000?'

'That's your first worry,' came the reply.

When Robert Maxwell met the Pope, the Holy Father asked him what he would have done if he'd been present at the Last Supper.

'Asked for separate bills,' said the fat man.

BARBER:

'Is it just a haircut you're wanting, Mr Maxwell, or shall I do an oil change, too?'

Robert Maxwell made the following declaration in his will: 'I want six directors of National Westminster Bank as pallbearers at my funeral. They've carried me so far, they might as well finish the job.'

A team of doctors was combing the grounds of Guy's Hospital, their eyes glued to the ground, seemingly searching every square inch.

'Excuse me,' said a visitor, 'but have you lost something?'

'No,' said one, 'we're doing a heart transplant for Robert Maxwell and we're looking for a suitable stone.'

What was the last thing to go through Robert Maxwell's mind when he fell off the boat?
The rudder.

Did you hear, Mrs Maxwell has had a bit of good news at last?
The rudder was insured.

What do you get if you cross the Atlantic with the *Lady Ghislaine*?
Halfway.

What was the difference between Robert Maxwell and a bucket of shit?
The bucket.

What do you call a dead newspaper proprietor floating in the ocean?
Bob.

TRUE STORY

Robert Maxwell threw a party for all *Mirror* employees shortly after he arrived as new proprietor. There was much food, drink, films and dancing, but the most talked-about sartorial note was undoubtedly Robert Maxwell's prominent corset.

It was discovered much later that Maxwell had paid for the party with money allowed by the Inland Revenue to cover employee Christmas entertainment. Immediately after the party he declared that no such allowance was to be given to the newspaper departments again, though he still, apparently, claimed the allowance from the taxman.

What had many legs and one fat arsehole?
The board of MCC.

Years back, Robert Maxwell was on the phone to the director of the cemetery at Mount Olive. The cost of a plot was £10,000, but Maxwell was not prepared to pay top whack. 'Why on earth not?' demanded the cemetery director. 'Because I'm only going to be there three days,' said Maxwell.

What would Robert Maxwell be doing today if he were alive?
    Scratching at the inside of his coffin.

What is Robert Maxwell doing these days?
    Decomposing.

THE END
(and that's final)